Young Boss – Math All Around Us

AN ENTREPRENERIAL WORKSHOP FOR YOUTH

Copyrighted 2015 by King Salute Foundation

Authors

Christopher Grant

Marcia Lawson

ISBN: 9798644050604

2nd Edition

May 2020

Table of Contents

Table of Contents 2

Workshop Introduction 3

and Expectations 3

Lesson 1: Gift/Talent Exploration and Identification 4

Gift/Talent Exploration vs Opportunity Mapping 6

Opportunity Selection 7

Lesson 2: Opportunity Exploration And Planning 8

Lesson 3: Product/Service Design And Test 12

Lesson 4: Product Launch And Review (Product Launch Sequence) 19

Lesson 5: Product/Service Sale And Delivery 23

Workshop Introduction and Expectations

Question: What is Young Boss – Math Around Us?

Answer: Young Boss is an entrepreneurial workshop for youth in Elementary, Middle and High school, geared to help students understand and apply fundamental mathematical concepts.

Question: Why Young Boss?

Answer: The Young Boss workshop is designed to help youth develop:

1. Clear goals
2. Character and leadership skills
3. Money and time management skills
4. Self esteem
5. A passion for serving others.
6. Apply mathematical concepts
7. Help secure America's future entrepreneurs

Lesson 1: Gift/Talent Exploration and Identification

Definition of an Entrepreneur:

Question: Who is an Entrepreneur?

Answer: _____

_____

Task 1: List five things you really like to do.

1.
2.
3.
4
5.

Task 2: List 3-5 ways you **THINK** you could help others by doing what you like to do.

1.
2.
3.
4.
5.

Task 3: Share task 2 list with fellow students and ask them if they have a need for what you like to do.

Keep score of each response with Y for YES and N for NO.

Ideas	YES Response	No Response
1.		
2.		
3.		
4.		
5.		

MATH SKILLS AT WORK:

Task 4: List 3 - 5 math skills that you need or can use to perform the tasks listed above in Task 2. *(Example, add, subtract, etc.)*

Ideas	Math Skills (3 – 5 for each)
1.	
2.	
3.	
4.	
5.	

Gift/Talent Exploration vs Opportunity Mapping

Task 5: Select top two things you like to do and that others need by counting all **YES'** for each idea on your list. State the numbers of Yes's for each.

List top 2 Ideas	YES Responses
1.	
2.	

Task 6: Ask fellow students if they would pay you for meeting their need(s).

List top 2 *Ideas*	YES Responses
1.	
2.	

Opportunity Selection

Task 7: Select the most popular thing you like to do that others would be willing to pay you for doing

List most popular *idea*	Write down how many YES

Lesson 2: Opportunity Exploration And Planning

Task 1: State your name and share the one thing most people would pay you for doing.

Hint (Lesson 1, Task 6)

Name:
Idea:

Task 2: Listen to instructor as he/she explain Business Model Canvas

Question: What is a Business Model Canvas?

Task 3: Work in groups and design a business model for a lemonade stand.

Notes: (Instructor will guide you as you complete each section. Do not write on Business Model Canvas. Write on sticky notes then transfer to Business Model Canvas). *Your business model canvas is provided on page 11.*

Task 4: Use the Business Model Canvas to create a business model for your idea. *Hint (task1)*

Notes: (Instructor will guide you as you complete each section. Do not write on Business Model Canvas. Write on sticky notes then transfer to Business Model Canvas)

Task 5: Share your business model with 2 other participants and ask for feedback

Feedback 1:

Feedback 2:

Task 6: Make changes based on feedback if necessary

What change(s) are you making?

What will that do for your idea?

MATH SKILLS AT WORK:

Task 7: List 3 - 5 math skills that you need or can use to perform the task(s) used in the business model, at least one skill should be different from the previous list. *(Example, add, subtract, etc.)*

Ideas	Math Skills (3 – 5 skill)
1.	
2.	
3.	
4.	
5.	

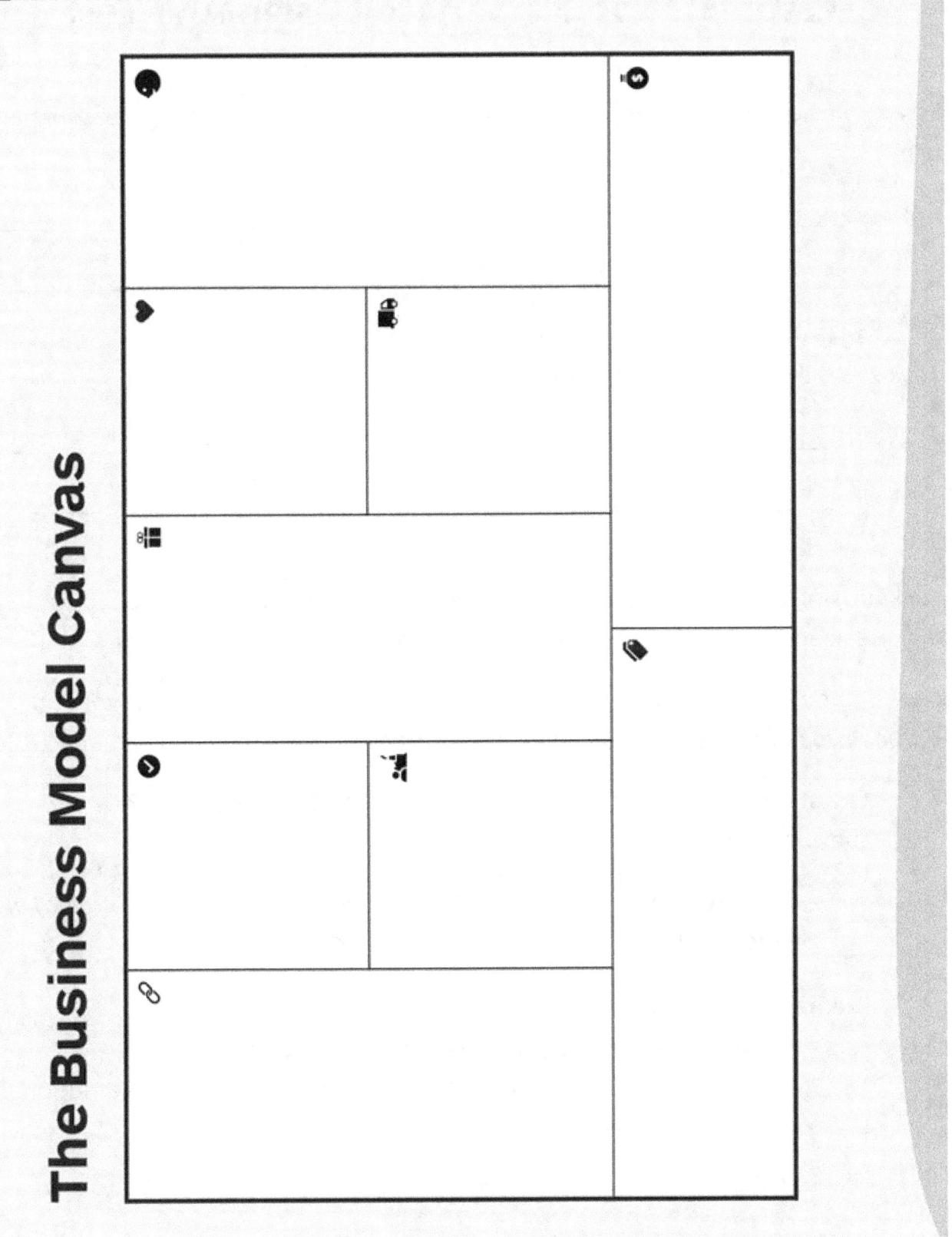

Lesson 3: Product/Service Design And Test

Task 1: Review the **Business Model Canvas**. List one component and describe its use?

Answer: _____

_____

Task 2: What is **Value Proposition**?

Answer: _____

_____

Task3: Using the lemonade stand example, design a product and or service by digging deeper to understand the customer's needs. *(Customer Profile)*

Notes: (Instructor will guide you as you complete each section. Do not write on **Value Proposition Design**. *You value proposition canvas is provided on page 18.*

> Question 1: Ask customer **what** job they are trying to get done? Or what they need? Make a list
>
> > *Hint: Need may be functional (practical), social (follow the crowd) or emotional (how you feel)*
>
> Example: I eat when I am hungry. --- Functional
> I eat because everyone else is eating. --- social
> I eat because I like how certain food makes me feel. --- emotional

Question 2: Ask customer **why** they need that job done?   Make a list.

Hint: **Why** *explain the customer's reason/purpose, (Ex. Pain, annoyance, avoidance, etc.)*

Question 3: Ask customer what would happen if they did not get needs met? Make a list

Hint: pain

Question 4: Ask customer how they are affected when they don't have what they need. Make a list

Hint: pain

[   ]

Question 5: Ask customer who else are affected when they don't have what they need. Make a list

   Hint: pain

[   ]

Question 6: Ask customer what would happen if they get what they need?

   Hint: gain

[   ]

Question 7: Ask customer who else is affected when they get what they need?

   Hint: gain

[   ]

Task 4: Using the lemonade stand example, design a product and or service by digging deeper to create value based on your understanding of customer needs

(Value Map)

Question 1: How can you provide value that **HELP'S** the customer gets the job done? Make a list.

Question 2: Create value that address' the customer's pains/fears. Make a list of how.

Hint: (pain releaser)

Question 3: Create value that address' the customer's gains. Make a list of how.

Hint: (gain creator)

Task 5: Test product/service design by matching **Value Map** with **Customer Profile**.

Question 1: How did you provide value that **HELP'S** the customer gets the job done? Make a list

Question 2: Does your proposed value address' the customer's pains/fears. Make a list of how

Hint: (pain releaser)

Question 3: Does your proposed value address' the customer's gains. Make a list of how

Hint: (gain creator)

Task 6: Plug value proposition back into business model canvas and see if anything changes

Task 7: Repeat the process for your business idea.

MATH SKILLS AT WORK:

Task 8: List 2 - 3 math skills that you need or can use to perform the tasks listed in your value map. *(Example, add, subtract, etc.)*

Ideas	Math Skills (3 – 5 for each)
1.	
2.	
3.	

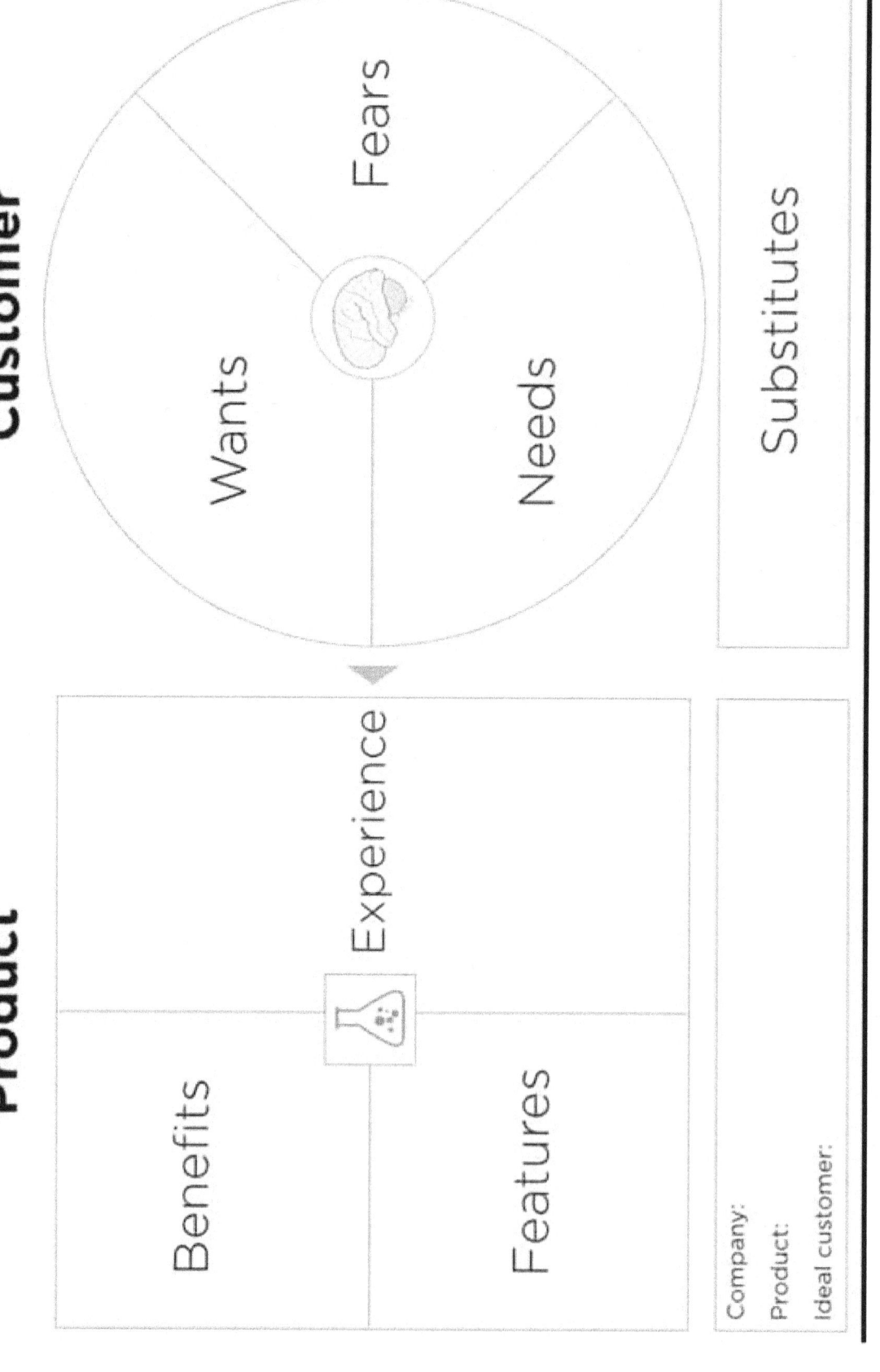

Lesson 4: Product Launch And Review (Product Launch Sequence)

Task 1: Review the **Business Model Canvas**. List one component and describe its use?

Task 2: **The 4 P'S** of marketing

1.
2.
3.
4.

Question 1. Explain your understanding of marketing? (Customer Centric Marketing)

Answer: _____

_____

Question 2: What is your favorite commercial and why?

Answer: _____

_____

Task 3: Let's watch a few commercials and hear what your peers have to say about them.

Question 1: What did you observe from watching these commercials?

Answer: _____

_____

Question 2: Did they tell the truth about what their product or service can do?

Answer: _____

_____

Question 3: What is the challenge with not telling the truth about what product/service you provide?

Answer: _____

_____

Task 4: Using the Lemonade Stand example; create marketing content that will appeal to the customer's needs. *(Use the **Value Proposition Design** to guide your creation of customer centric marketing content)*

Notes: *(Instructor will guide you as you complete each section. Do not write on **Business Model Canvas**. Write on sticky notes then transfer to **Business Model Canvas**)*

Question 1: What product/service are you offering potential clients as value? **(PRODUCT)**

Answer: _____

_____

Question 2: What is the price of your product or service? **(PRICE)**

Answer: _____

_____

Question 3: How will you send your message out? **(PROMOTIONS)**

Answer: _____

_____

Hint: ads, public relations, social media, email, search engine, video marketing

Question 4: What is the best place to put your product/service to engage potential customer? **(PLACE)**

Answer: _____

_____

Task 5: Write marketing material telling customers what value you have created for them.

Answer: _____

_____

_____

_____

Task 6: Insert marketing content in **Customer Relations** section and compare with **Value Proposition** to see if messaging and proposed value matches.

Task 7: Share with the class and ask for feedback.

Task 8: Repeat the process for your business idea.

Task 9: Go around the room, interact with each other and share your proposed value.

Task 10: Pick up the phone and share your proposed value with a customer

Task 11: Prepare and share your proposed value using audio.

Task 12: Prepare and share your proposed value using video.

Task 13: Compare the effectiveness of the different methods.

MATH SKILLS AT WORK:

Task 14: List 2 - 3 math skills that you need or can use to perform the tasks listed in your business model, pricing structure and customer relations tasks. *(Example, add, subtract, etc.)*

Ideas	Math Skills *(3 – 5 skills)*
1.	
2.	
3.	

Lesson 5: Product/Service Sale And Delivery

Question: What is selling?

Answer: _____

_____

Question: What is delivery?

Answer: _____

_____

Combine the responses above to create a definition for selling and delivery

Answer: _____

_____

Task 1: Ensure product/service is ready for customer to purchase

    Question 1: Is product packaging and presentation pleasing to the senses?

    Answer: _____

    _____

    Question 2: Will product/service give client desired response?

    Answer: _____

    _____

Task 2: Two methods of selling.
    Hint: A-I-D-A or 4 P'S of selling.

1.
2.

Task 3: Give examples of attention getting technique.

Make a list, and share

Task 4: Give examples of interest getting technique. *(WIIFM-what's in it for me.)*
Make a list, and share

Task 5: Give examples of getting someone emotionally involve.

Make a list, and share

Task 6: Give examples of a call to action.

Make a list, and share

Task 7: Make a math skill used as well as any new skills developed over the workshop. Share your list.

Task 8: Write a skit using all four components for Lemonade stand idea.

Hint: chose one item from each list. Ex. (Attention-interest-desire-action)

Task 9: Share with class and ask for feedback.

Task 10: Write a skit using all four components for your idea.

Task 11: Share with class and ask for feedback.

www.ingramcontent.com/pod-product-compliance
Lightning Source LLC
Chambersburg PA
CBHW081101240526
45465CB00025B/2811